ILLUMINATION PRESENTS

MEGA COLOURING

THE SECRET LIFE OF PETS: **MEGA COLOURING**
A CENTUM BOOK 9781910917831
Published in Great Britain by Centum Books Ltd
This edition published 2016
© 2016 Universal Studios Licensing LLC.
1 3 5 7 9 10 8 6 4 2

The Secret Life of Pets is a trademark and copyright of Universal Studios.
Licensed by Universal Studios LLC. All rights reserved.

UNIVERSAL.
A COMCAST COMPANY

Centum Books Ltd, 20 Devon Square, Newton Abbot, Devon, TQ12 2HR, UK
books@centumbooksltd.co.uk
CENTUM BOOKS Limited Reg. No. 07641486
A CIP catalogue record for this book is available from the British Library
Printed in China.

Centum

Max is one lucky dog. He lives in an apartment building in New York City with his other pet pals.

Look up, down, forwards and backwards to find
the names of Max and his friends.

R D U K E N D S F
L R I B N D L E M
E I F U O F S I A
O E D N R R F R X
N N S D M I N D N
A D N Y A C L I E
R S E S N E F R I
D I D C H L O E R
R E S T E G D I G

Mel

Leonard

Norman

Chloe

Gidget

Duke

Max

Max loves his human, Katie.

He waits all day for her to come home.

Max wishes Katie were at home to play with him.

Max and Katie are two of a kind.

Max and Katie like to go for rides.

Katie adopts Duke. He is now Max's new brother.

Look at the top picture carefully.
Then circle five things that are different in the bottom picture.

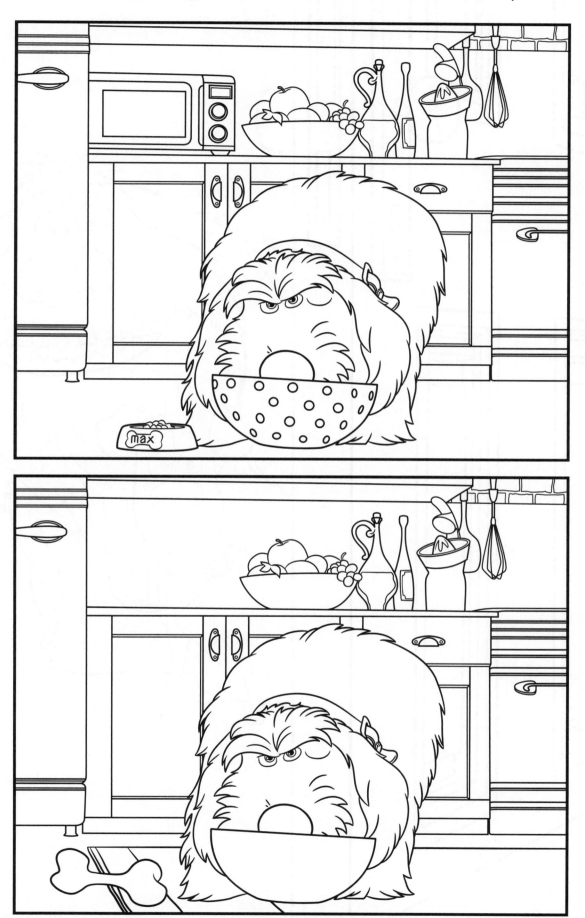

Max doesn't want Katie to leave him alone with Duke.

Duke plays fetch with Max.

Duke is excited about his new home, but Max isn't ready to share.

Duke wants Max's bone.
Solve the maze to help him get it.

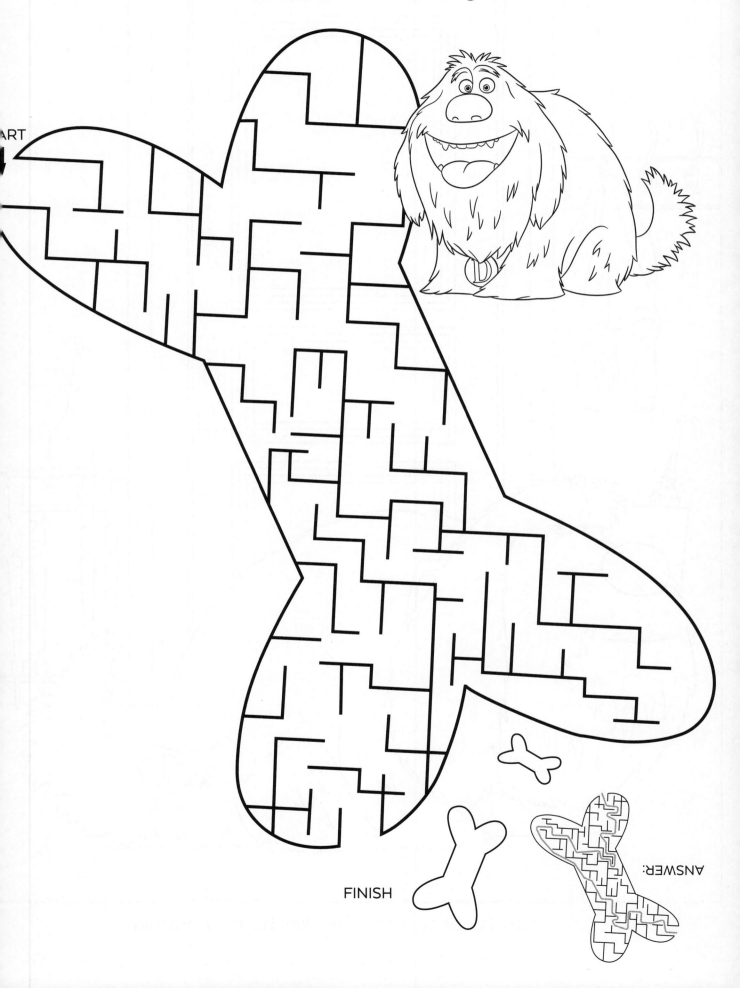

ART

FINISH

ANSWER:

Max is not sure that he likes his new brother.

Gidget is Max's next door neighbour.

Gidget is a cute Pomeranian. She fits in a handbag.

Gidget loves Max. She stares at him all day.

Sweetpea thinks he is one tough bird.

Mel is a friendly pug. He is happy at home.

Use the code below to find out what Mel likes to chase.

_ _ _ _ _ _ _ _

L=    S=   Q=   U=

I=   R=   E=   P=

Norman the guinea pig always gets lost.
Solve the maze by following only Norman.

Use the key to colour Norman.
(Key: 1=Brown 2=Black 3=Pink 4=White)

One of Chloe's favourite foods is cake!

Connect the dots to see what Chloe will eat next.
Then colour it in.

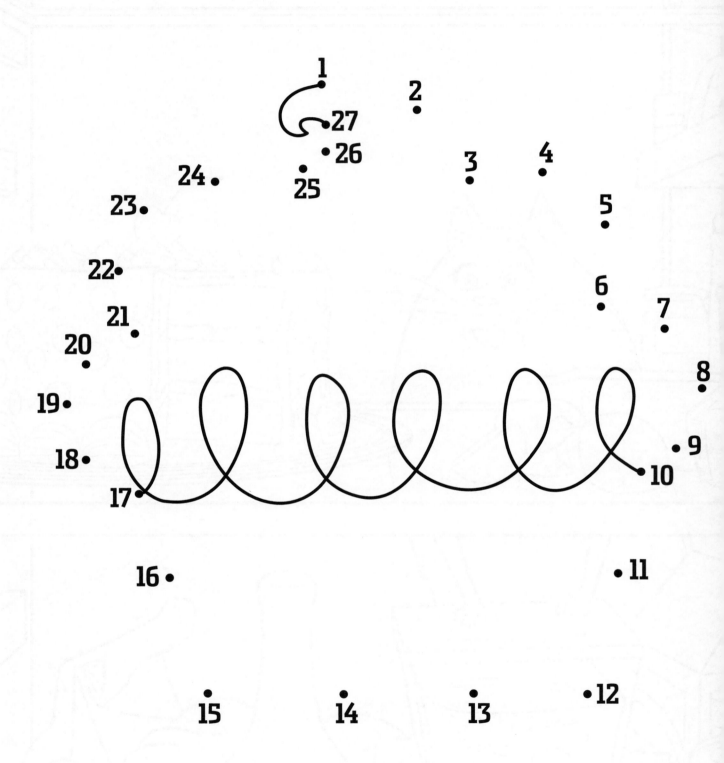

What are your favourite foods? Draw them here for Chloe.

To find out the name of this heavy-metal mutt,
follow the lines and write each letter on the correct blank.

E   R   D   O   L   N   A

—   —   —   —   —   —   —   —

Buddy likes to get a massage while his owner is away.

Max and his friends go for a walk in the park.

Mel chases a squirrel to the top of a tree.
Solve the maze.

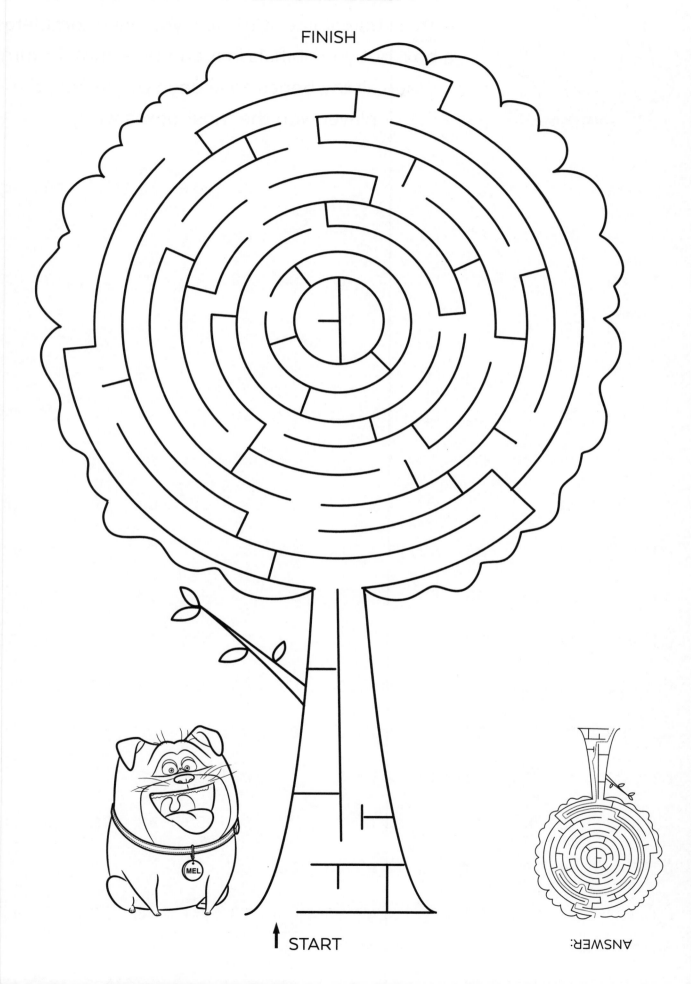

FINISH

START

MAX AND DUKE BOTH WANT TO BE TOP DOG.

With a friend, take turns connecting two bones with a straight line. If the line you draw completes a box, put your initials in it and take another turn. When all the bones have been connected, the player with the most boxes wins!

CUPCAKE SQUARE GAME.

With a friend, take turns connecting two cupakes with a straight line. If the line you draw completes a box, put your initials in it and take another turn. When all the cupcakes have been connected, the player with more boxes wins! The winner gets to colour in the big cupcake.

Match each pet to its shadow.

1

2

3

4

A

B

C

D

Look at the top picture carefully.

Then circle five things that are different in the bottom picture.

ANSWER: Some buildings are missing behind Gidget, Chloe's stripes are missing, Gidget's bow is missing, Mel's name is missing from his dog tag, and Duke's eyebrows are different.

These cats hang out all day. How many cats can you count?

Duke does not want to fetch a stick for Max.

Max and Duke get lost in the city and meet a mean cat.
To find out the cat's name, follow the lines from the letters and
write each letter on the dashes below.

O   N   O   E   Z

—   —   —   —   —

Ozone and his pals go after Max and Duke.

Ozone and his gang chase Max and Duke.
Solve the maze to help them escape.

START

FINISH

ANSWER:

Max and Duke meet another animal.
Connect the dots to reveal who it is.

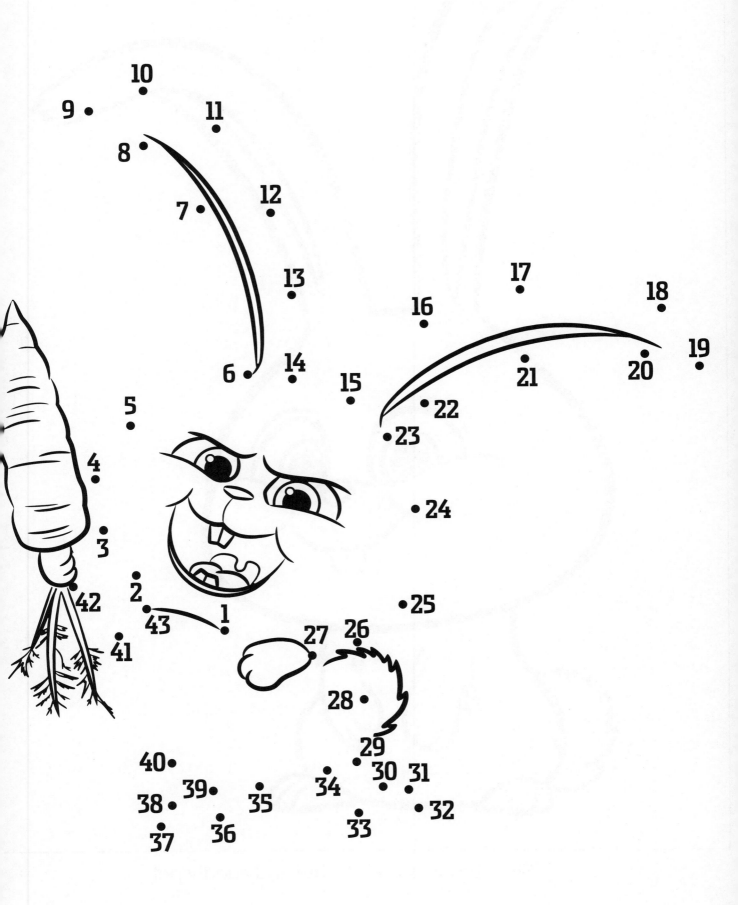

Snowball was once a cute and cuddly pet.

Snowball became the leader of the Flushed Pets.

Snowball has a message for pets everywhere.
To find out what it is, start at the arrow and, going clockwise
around the circle, write each letter in order on the blanks.

__ __ __ __ __ __ __ __ __

__ __ __ __ __ __ __ __ ,

__ __ __ __ __ __ __ __ __ __ __ __

__ __ __ __ __ __ !

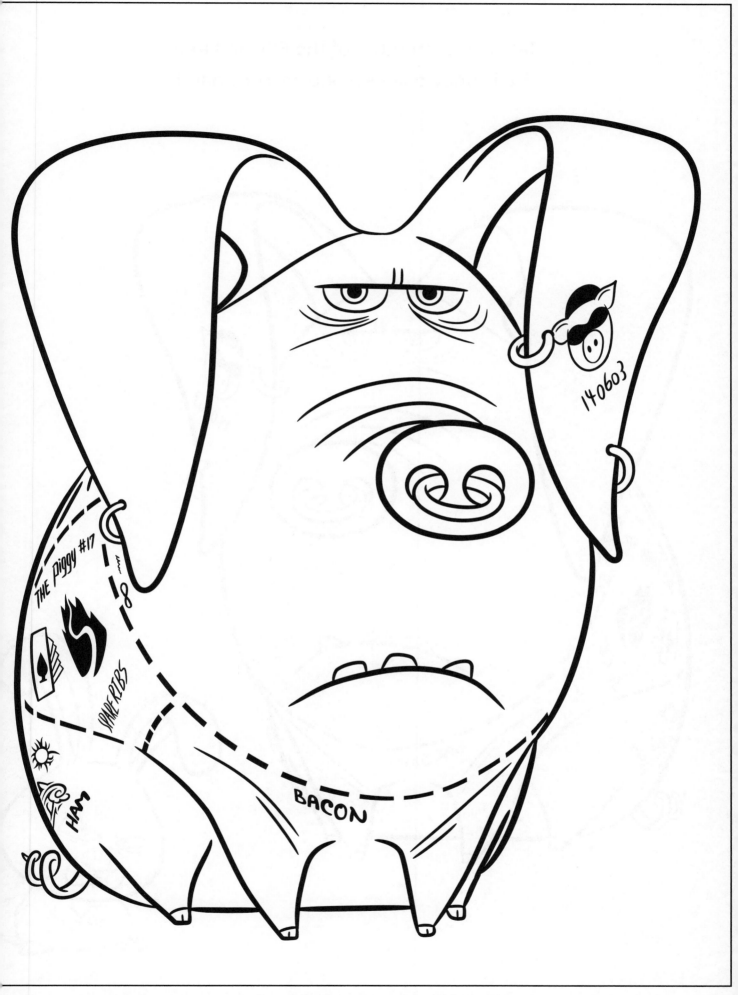

Tattoo's owners practised drawing their tattoos on him.

Tattoo is a member of the Flushed Pets.
He is Snowball's second-in-command.

How many words can you create from the letters in
'FLUSHED PETS'?

_____   _____

_____   _____

_____   _____

_____   _____

_____   _____

_____   _____

_____   _____

_____   _____

Use the grid below to draw a picture of Snowball.

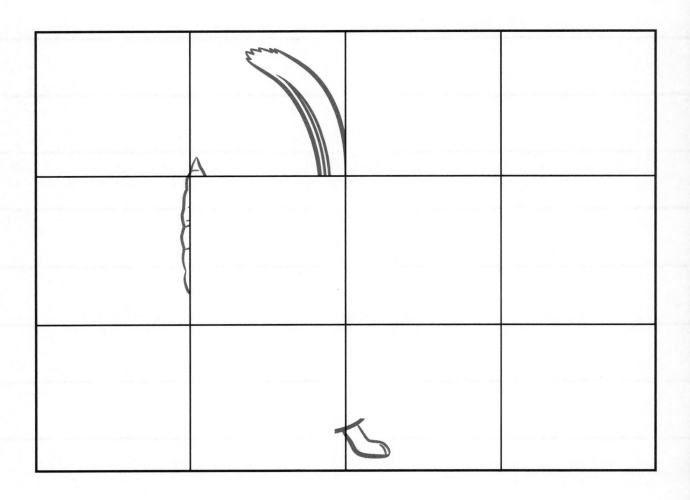

Can you find the two images of Snowball that are the same?

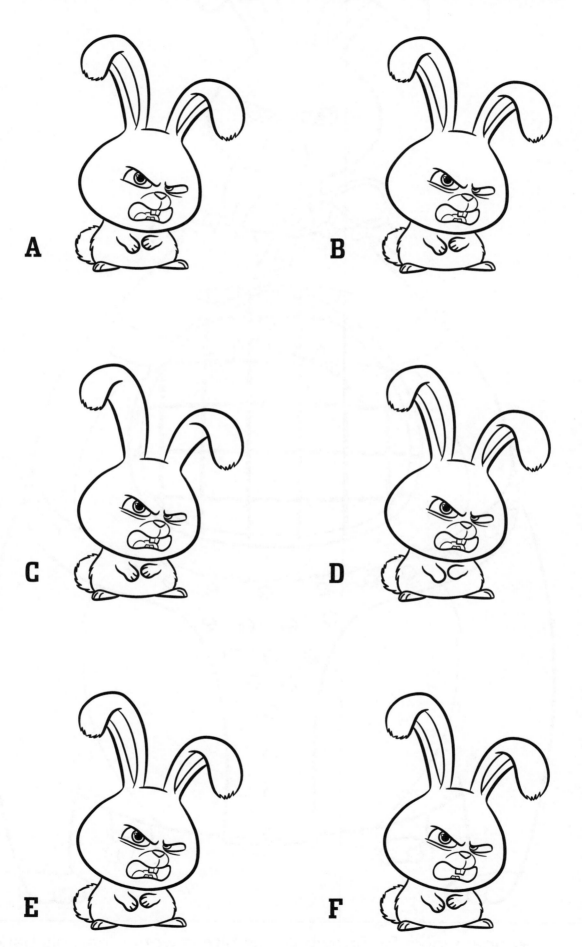

A

B

C

D

E

F

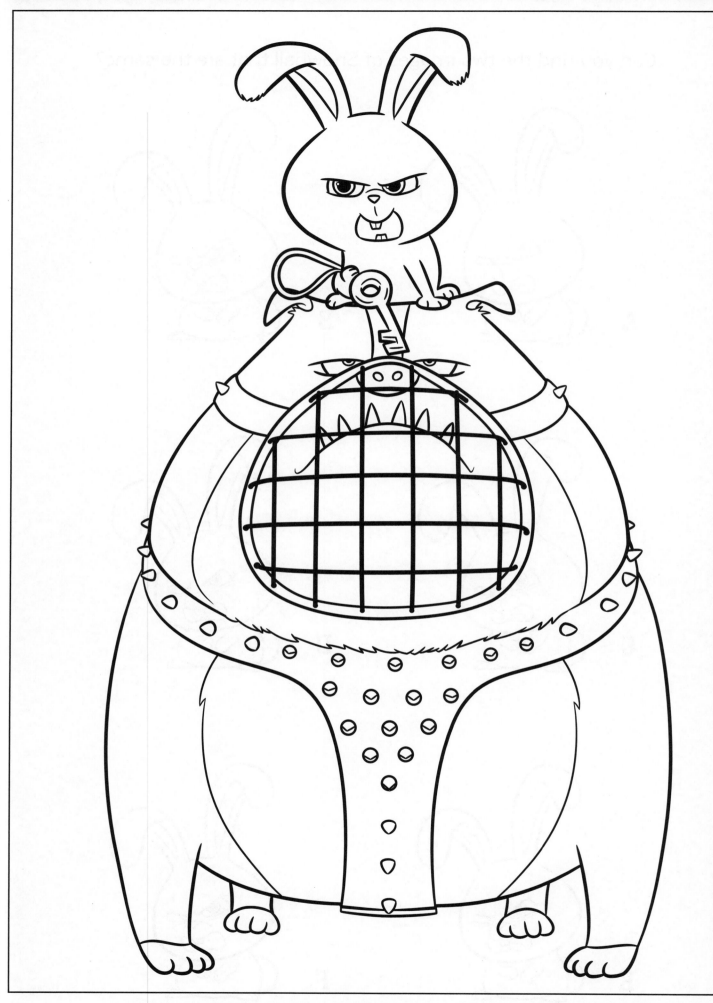

Ripper works for Snowball. His bite is worse than his bark.

How many times can you find the name 'RIPPER' in the puzzle below?

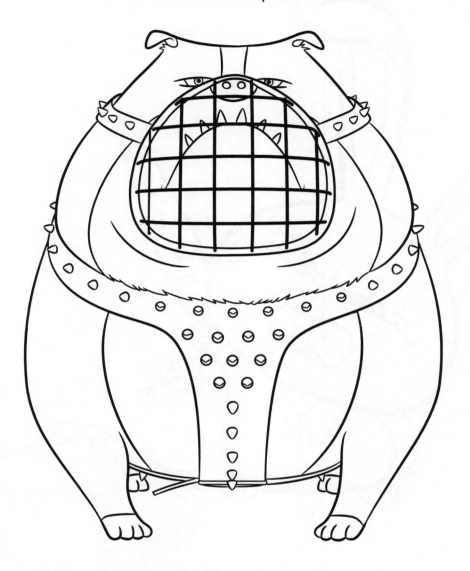

R E R E P P I R
I P P I R I E I
P I R R I P R P
P R I I P P E R
E R P P P R I E
R I P P E R E P
P I R E P E P P
I P E R P R I I
R I P P E I P R

Bearded Dragon is one of Snowball's henchmen.

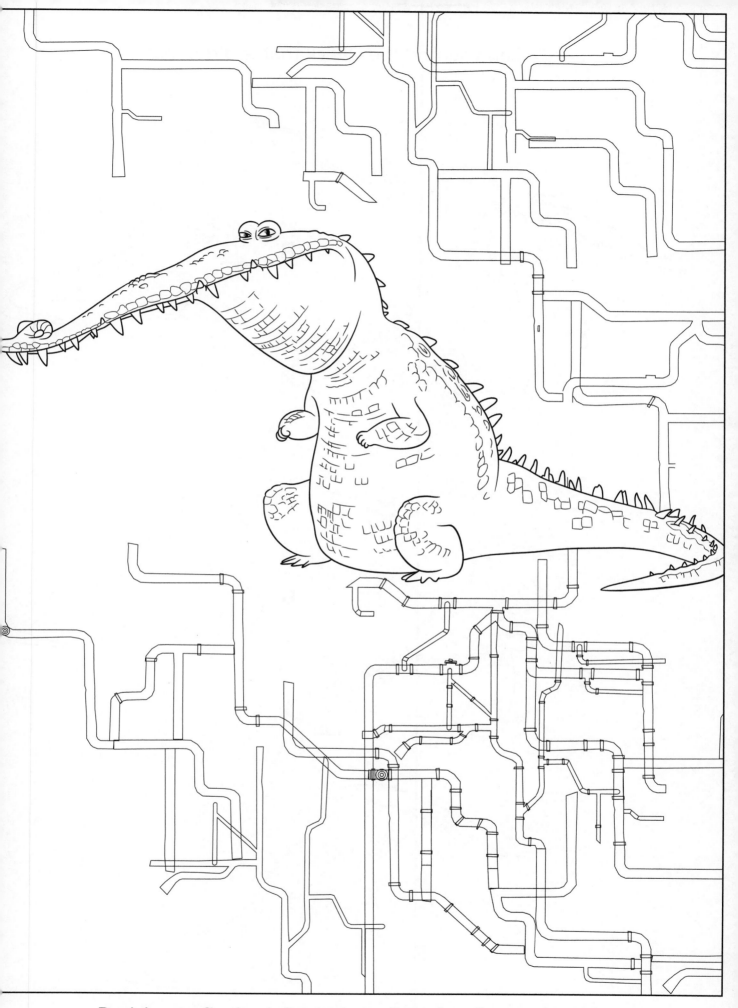

Derick was flushed down the toilet when he got too big.

Now he works for Snowball.

Can you find the Derick that is different?

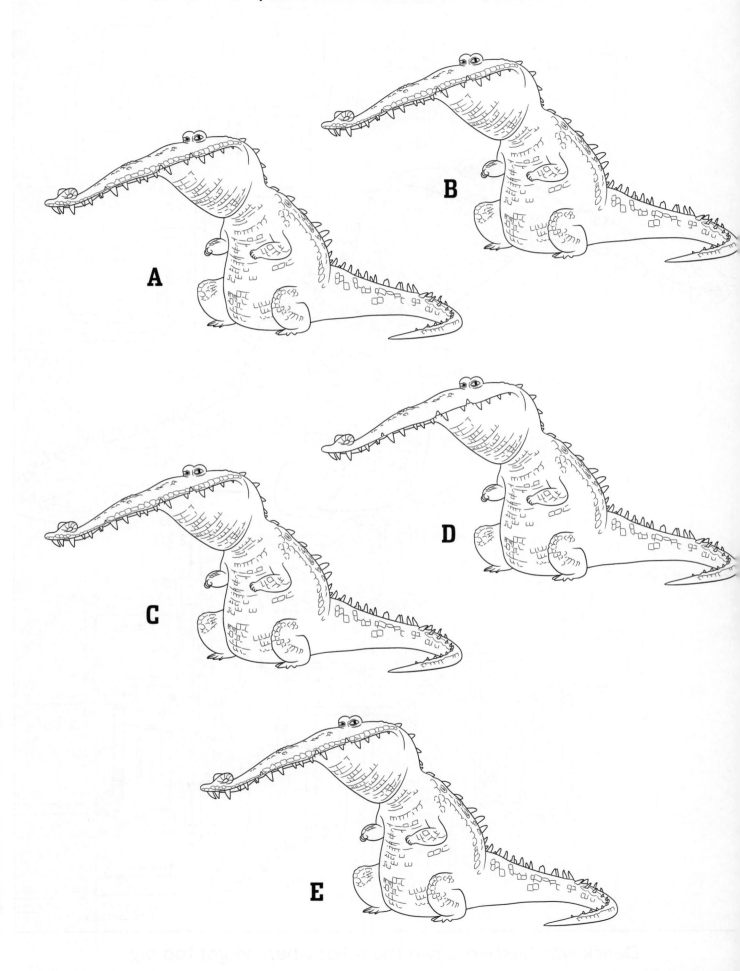

A

B

C

D

E

The Flushed Pets live in a secret place.
Use this key to find out what it's called.

ANSWER: Underbelly.

Y=  D= R= B=

U=  N= E= L=

Look at the top picture carefully.
Then circle five things that are different in the bottom picture.

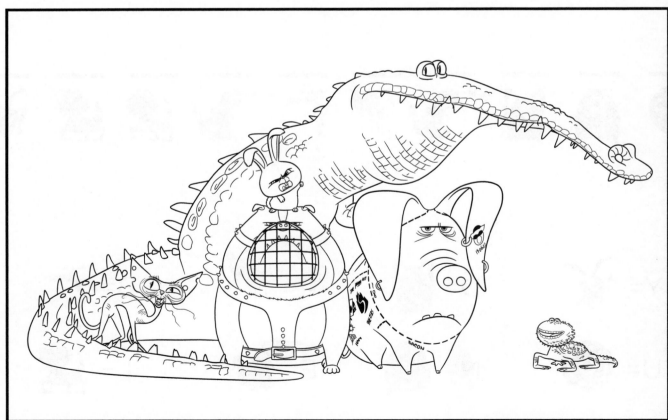

Gidget discovers that Max is missing.
She asks a hawk named Tiberius to help her.

No one messes with Gidget.

Solve the maze to help Gidget and the gang find Max and Duke.

START

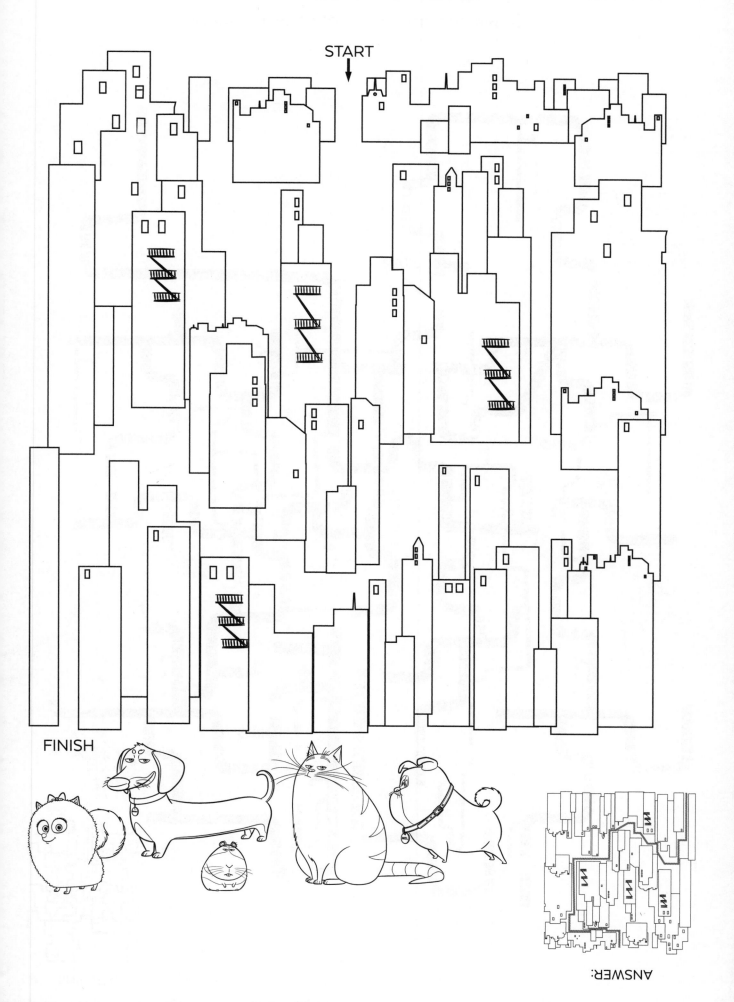

FINISH

ANSWER:

Max and Duke are trying to get away from the Flushed Pets.
Solve the maze to help them escape.

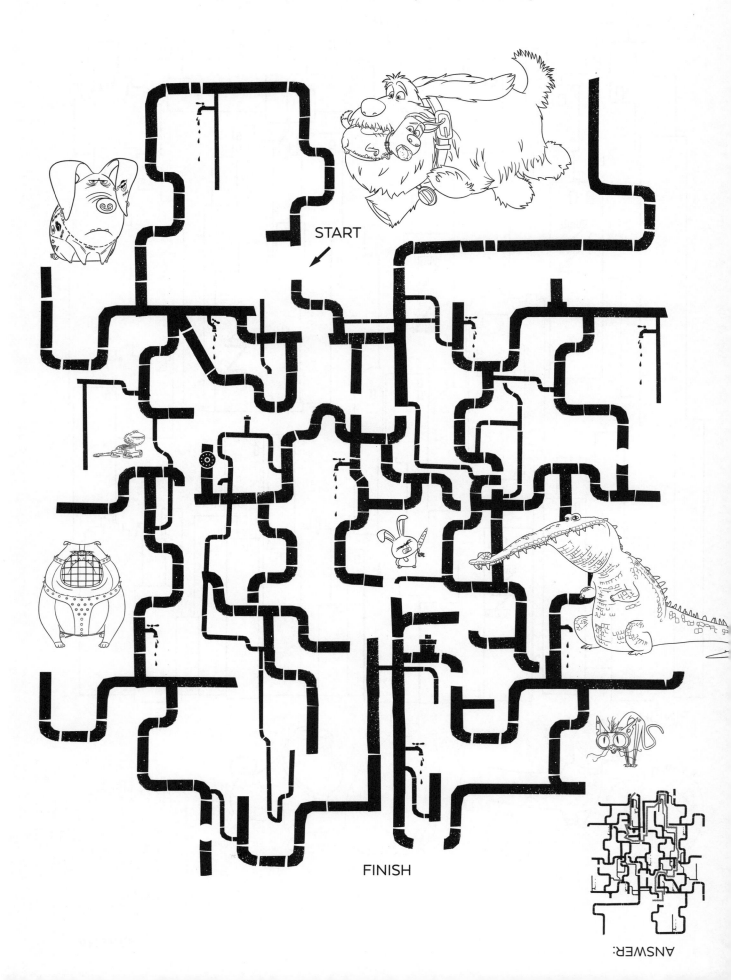

START

FINISH

Max and Duke love sausages.
How many sausages can you count?

Find the path that leads Max and Duke out of the sausage factory.

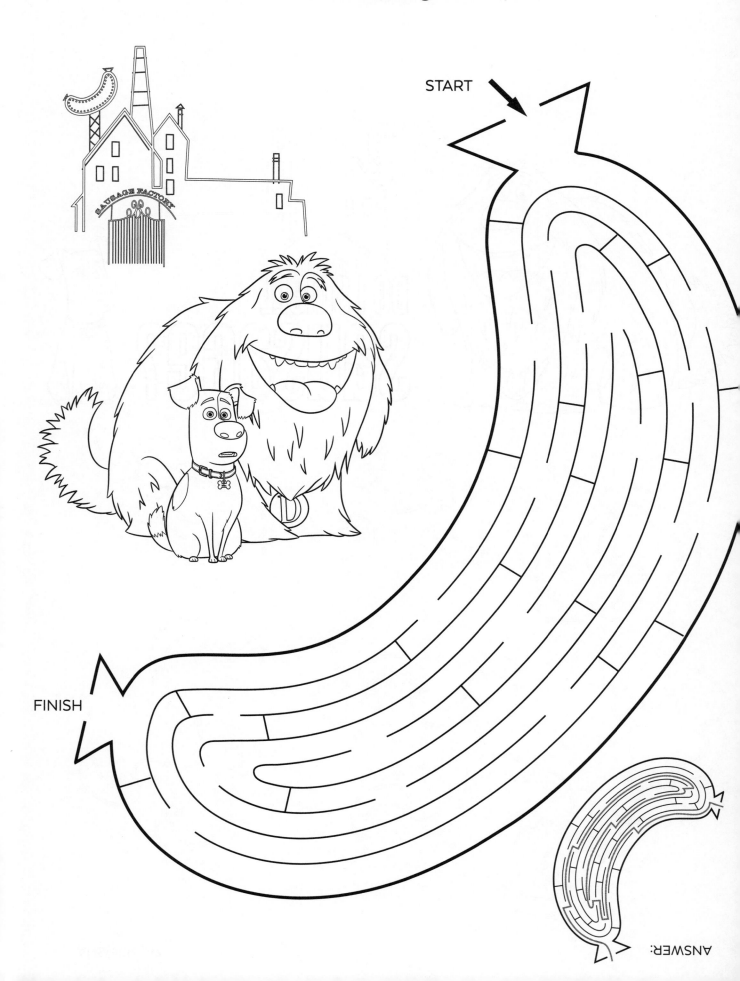

START

FINISH

SAUSAGE FACTORY

ANSWER:

Which shadow matches the image of Max and Duke in the basket?

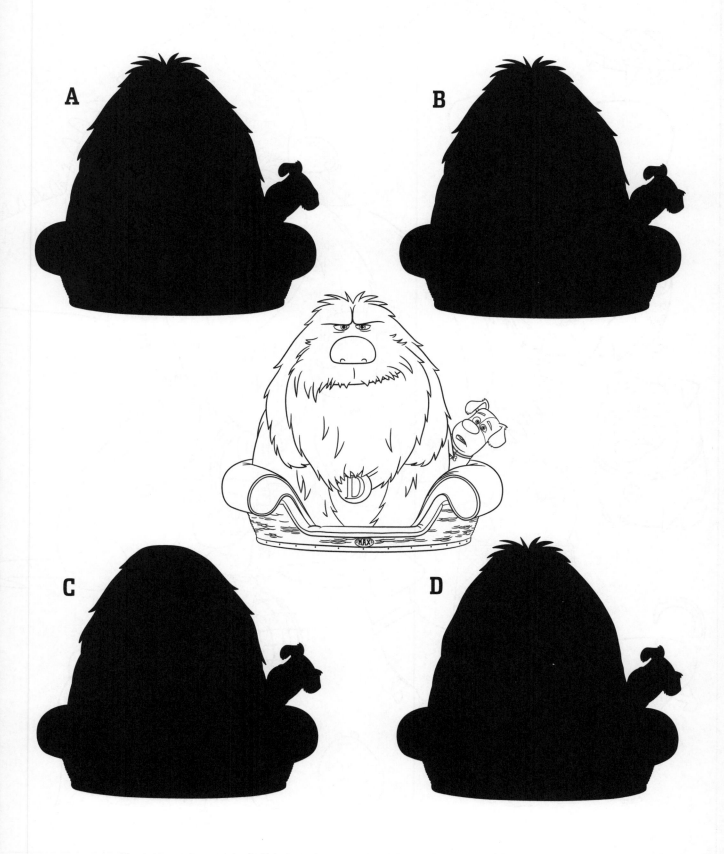

A

B

C

D

The Flushed Pets are very different from Max and his friends.

Use the code below to find out the Pets' worst enemy.

___ ___ ___ ___ ___ ___

A= M= N=

I= L= O=

C= R= T=

How many times can you find the word FRIENDS in the puzzle?
Look up, down, forwards and backwards.

```
R F R I E N D S   F
F R I E N D S E   R
I I F R I F S I   S
E E D F E R F R   D
N N S I F I N D   N
S D N E I R F S   E
D S E S R E F R   I
F I D D D N I E   R
R E S D N E I R   F
```